™BREATHINGBOOK

Euphonium Edition

David Vining

Preface by Patrick Sheridan

The Breathing Book
Euphonium Edition
David Vining
MPM 15-001
$19.95

© 2009 Mountain Peak Music

2700 Woodlands Village Blvd. #300-124
Flagstaff, Arizona 86001
www.mountainpeakmusic.com

This publication is protected by Copyright Law.
Do not photocopy. All rights reserved.

ISBN 978-1-935510-02-4

THE BREATHING BOOK

Preface i

Introduction ii

1. Be Balanced 1

2. Be a Bobblehead 3

3. Know Where the Air Goes 5

4. Move Your Ribs 7

5. Allow Your Spine to Gather and Lengthen 9

6. The Truth About the Diaphragm 11

7. Feel Support from Your Pelvic Floor 13

8. Exhalation and Elastic Recoil 15

9a. Breathe All Over – Low Range 17

9b. Breathe All Over – High Range 19

10. Let the Air Drive Your Tongue 21

11a. Blow Freely as You Change Notes – Slow 23

11b. Blow Freely as You Change Notes – Fast 25

12. Quality of Effort and the Valsalva Maneuver ... 27

13. Monitor Your Air Gauge 29

Summary 31

Flow Study 32

Preface

THE BREATHING BOOK

Imagine for a moment what your favorite brass players look like when they perform on their instruments. They look relaxed. They look tensionless. Everything appears easy. The music flows out of the performer gracefully and reaches the listener in a way that leaves them changed forever by the beauty of the song. The performer is free of any physical bonds and can concentrate on delivering the message of the music.

As a young developing brass player I remember feeling inundated with phrases and tips about what to do with my body when I was playing my instrument, particularly as it related to breathing. I remember phrases like "Breathe low" and "Breathe from the bottom", etc. Occasionally these types of instructions made sense to me and helped briefly. More often though, phrases like these confused me. Often I felt as though the intent of the instructional phrase was working against what my body wanted to do naturally. When this was the case, playing was hard. It was filled with tension and my sound reflected that tension. In these moments, there was no joy associated with playing my instrument.

Indeed, for many years, the standard view of the function of the body during breathing was based on how the body looked from the outside. This book views the body from the inside—showing pictures of the structures of the body related to breathing and how the proper function of these structures can work to help us breathe freely.

More importantly—beyond Mr. Vining's clear and concise explanations of these breathing structures—he has developed specific playing activities for each breathing structure area that help us experience proper breathing function. These activities simply and effectively give us a pathway to experience breathing (and thereby performing) in a free and easy way. Great breathing leads to great music on a wind instrument. It is here we find joyful music making!!

This book is a fantastic guide for any brass player to understand their body's respiratory function. Further, the information presented here offers healthy and safe recommendations for playing development. Bravo, David Vining, for bringing brass pedagogy the information necessary to free our breathing and clear the obstacles which stand in the way of wonderful music making!

All the best,

Patrick Sheridan

Co-Author, *The Breathing Gym*

Introduction

Musicians move to make music. When a euphonium player plays, there are many movements which must be coordinated in order to create the desired sound: the fingers must move with precision to ensure excellent technique; the tongue must move appropriately to articulate cleanly; the embouchure must move properly to produce the right pitch. Euphonium players must also move air to create a resonant tone quality and the movement of the air comes from the breath support.

The quality of a euphonium player's movements determines the quality of the sound. For example, euphonium players with precise tongue motions play with excellent articulations, and euphonium players with inexact tongue motions play with poor articulations. Similarly, euphonium players who breathe well create a resonant tone quality and euphonium players who do not breathe well lack resonance.

To breathe well means to breathe free of tension, and tension-free breathing occurs when we move in cooperation with how we are built. In other words, if we know how we are supposed to move to breathe, we will move freely and our sound will be resonant. If our movements do not cooperate with the reality of how we are built, our sound will be full of tension and our resonance will suffer.

Knowing about breathing movements is just like knowing about music theory or music history. Our knowledge of theory and history informs our playing and serves as a foundation upon which we can make educated musical decisions. Similarly, our understanding of breathing informs our playing and serves as a foundation upon which our music-making movements occur. A detailed understanding of theory and history provides a strong musical foundation, enabling us to make informed musical decisions. A detailed understanding of the movements of breathing provides a strong movement foundation, enabling us to breathe free of tension and to create the resonance we seek. After all, since euphonium players move to make music, it makes sense to understand how to move every bit as much as it makes sense to understand how to spell chords.

When we perform, our knowledge of theory and history is not foremost in our thinking. It exists in the background, rather like the foundation of a house. Likewise, once we learn about the movements of breathing, this knowledge exists in the background, right alongside our knowledge of theory and history. It is not necessary (or helpful) to walk out on stage thinking about your diaphragm as you are about to perform!

If our knowledge of music history and music theory is inaccurate, our musical decision-making is impaired. Correspondingly, if our knowledge of breathing is inaccurate, our ability to breathe free of tension is impaired. As we learn to play euphonium, sometimes we learn how to breathe metaphorically and the metaphors do not always cooperate with reality. The metaphors can create misunderstandings which cause tension in our breathing. This book is designed to teach the truth about breathing, so we can breathe free of tension. It is a book full of movement facts, not metaphors. It is a movement book, not an exercise book.

Each section in this book includes an important breathing fact with an image on the left page and a playing activity on the right page. For maximum benefit, think about the movement facts as you play the activity and you will integrate the knowledge into your playing in meaningful ways. Learn the movement facts well enough so they become part of your musical foundation, and eventually, there will be no need to focus on the breathing movements as you play. The best musicians breathe well without focusing on their breathing and devote their attention to musical thoughts as they perform.

1. Be Balanced

All of the individual movements of breathing coalesce into the singular, well coordinated and organic motion of breathing. The motion of breathing is complex but it needn't be confusing, because ultimately, musicians need only cooperate with nature to breathe well. The only improvements to be made are in our cooperation with the process.

In order to breathe well, it is important to achieve muscular freedom throughout your body. One of the keys to achieving muscular freedom is to allow your bony structure to hold up your body. Your skeleton is designed to deliver your weight to the chair or floor in cooperation with gravity, and when you rely upon your bones in this way, you are balanced. There is no need to use muscular work to hold yourself up when you are balanced.

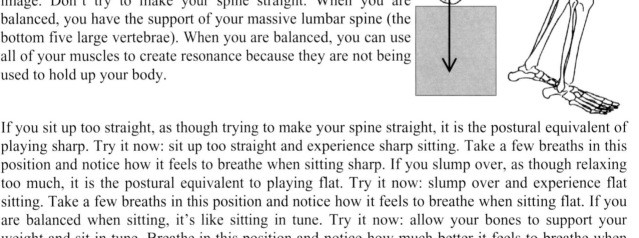

Balance is an internal, lively sensation, not the stagnant holding of a position. You can feel whether or not you are balanced when you have musical movement available to you in any direction. Try it now: as you observe the image, allow your weight to be delivered down to your chair and move in little circles on your rockers. Your rockers are the two rounded bones which make contact with your chair. Notice from the image that you don't sit on your legs; they attach to your pelvis above your rockers.

When you are balanced, your spine will be curved, as in the image. Don't try to make your spine straight. When you are balanced, you have the support of your massive lumbar spine (the bottom five large vertebrae). When you are balanced, you can use all of your muscles to create resonance because they are not being used to hold up your body.

If you sit up too straight, as though trying to make your spine straight, it is the postural equivalent of playing sharp. Try it now: sit up too straight and experience sharp sitting. Take a few breaths in this position and notice how it feels to breathe when sitting sharp. If you slump over, as though relaxing too much, it is the postural equivalent to playing flat. Try it now: slump over and experience flat sitting. Take a few breaths in this position and notice how it feels to breathe when sitting flat. If you are balanced when sitting, it's like sitting in tune. Try it now: allow your bones to support your weight and sit in tune. Breathe in this position and notice how much better it feels to breathe when sitting in tune.

Notice that being balanced is a prerequisite to breathing well. Being balanced is like being in tune—it makes everything else about your playing easier!

2. Be a Bobblehead

The average head weighs anywhere from eight to twelve pounds, about the same as a bowling ball. Imagine holding up a bowling ball as you try to play your instrument!

Fortunately, your skeleton and your dynamic balance mechanism are designed to hold up your head for you if you are balanced, as discussed in chapter one. You have a special joint where your skull is poised atop your spine called the atlanto-occipital, or AO joint, and it is directly between your ears. Find the joint now: point your index fingers directly into your ear holes, making sure your fingers are parallel to the ground—you are now pointing toward the joint. As you are pointing toward your AO joint with your fingers, move your skull in little bobblehead movements, right at the joint, not lower.

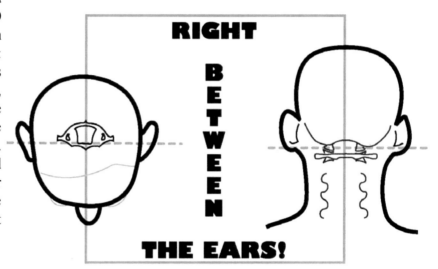

Being a bobblehead is part of being balanced. If we allow the weight of our head to be delivered downward in cooperation with gravity, the weight passes directly through our AO joint. This is important because if the weight of our head is dragged forward of the joint or pushed backward behind the joint, we are required to use our neck muscles to hold up the weight. This neck tension adversely affects our tone quality and other aspects of our playing. Temporary movements away from balance as you move with the music are certainly beneficial, but chronic imbalance of the head should not be confused with temporary musical movements.

You can also be a bobblehead as you play, in which case your free neck ensures a free tone quality. Try it now: while sitting in a balanced position with your instrument down, move like a bobblehead—in little circles at your AO joint. Now bring your instrument up into playing position *as you continue the movements.* Did you drag your head forward to meet your euphonium? You shouldn't! Never move your body to meet the instrument; always bring the instrument to your body so your balance is not compromised.

You can use subtle bobblehead movements to "check in" with your balance. Any time you feel tense as you play, move like a bobblehead, right from the AO joint. The movements can be so small that nobody sees them, even though you feel them!

2. Be a Bobblehead

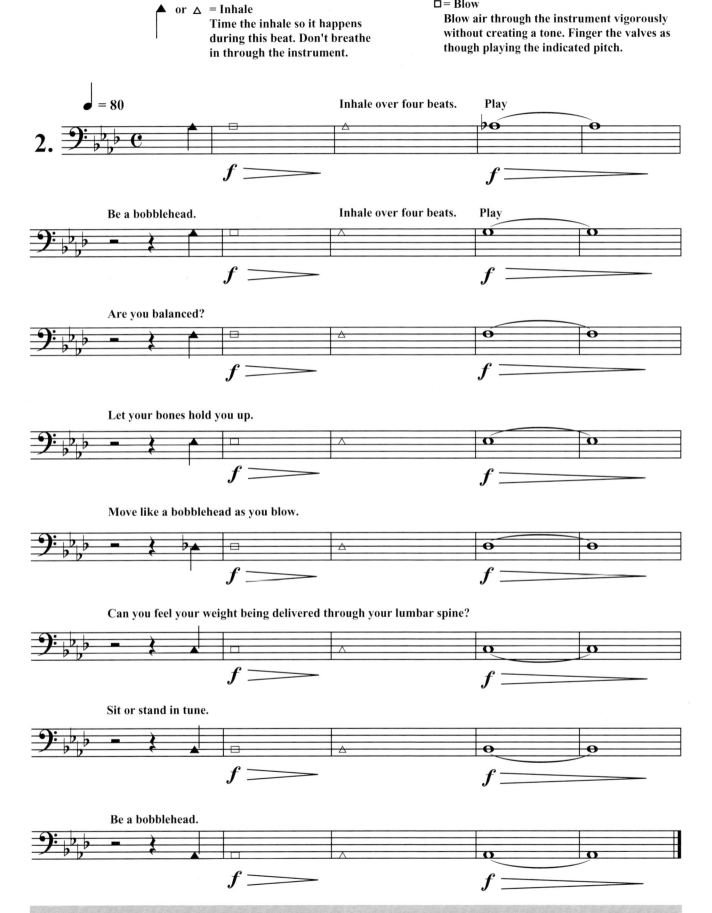

3. Know Where the Air Goes

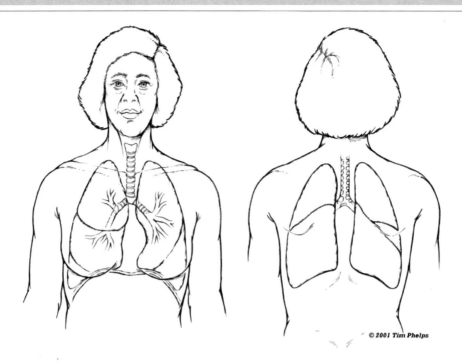

As you can see in this image, your lungs extend above your collarbones. Take a moment now to touch your collarbones with your fingertips in order to clarify the position of the tops of your lungs. While looking at the illustration, move your fingertips onto the soft tissue above your collarbones and in front of the lung tissue so that your fingertips can help you understand that the lungs come up that high in your body. You may need to do this many times a day if you have mapped your lungs as being lower in the body.

Now tap on your sternum (or breast bone) moving downward until you find where it ends. As you touch this spot, you are near the bottoms of your lungs in front. If you look at the picture, you will see they lie lower in the back. This is where the air goes. Now touch the tube which delivers the air to your lungs. It is called the trachea and it can be felt easily in the front of your neck. View the image as you touch your trachea and notice that it consists of rings of cartilage which you can feel. This construction ensures that the trachea remains open at all times. As you inhale, there is no need to use muscular effort to hold the trachea open, as so many players try to do.

As you can see in the image, the trachea divides into two tubes to deliver air to each of your lungs. The tubes then divide again and again, getting smaller and smaller in order to distribute the air to the bloodstream efficiently. When you inhale, the air goes to all parts of the lungs equally; it does not go to the bottoms of the lungs first, as though it were water.

Air does not go down to your bellybutton. Your conception of where the air goes will determine how your body moves; if you think the air goes down by your bellybutton then your belly will move to match that idea. This sort of aberrant breathing movement looks rather like belly dancing breathing—don't be a belly dancing breather because it will interfere with your playing!

3. Know Where the Air Goes

Before you begin, look at the image on the previous page and clarify the position of your lungs in your body.

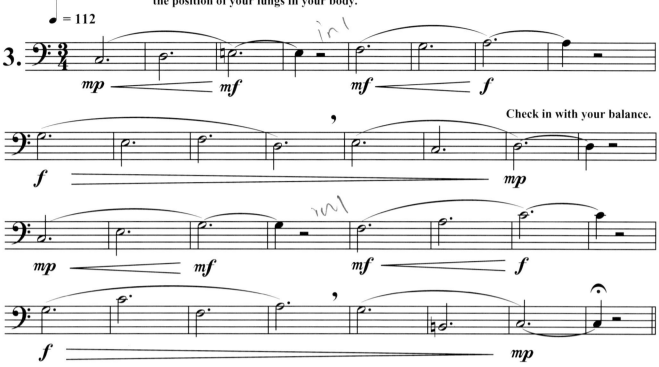

Check in with your balance.

**During the rest, view the image once again to clarify the position of the lungs in the body.
As you play the remainder of this activity, breathe with a clear understanding of where the air goes.**

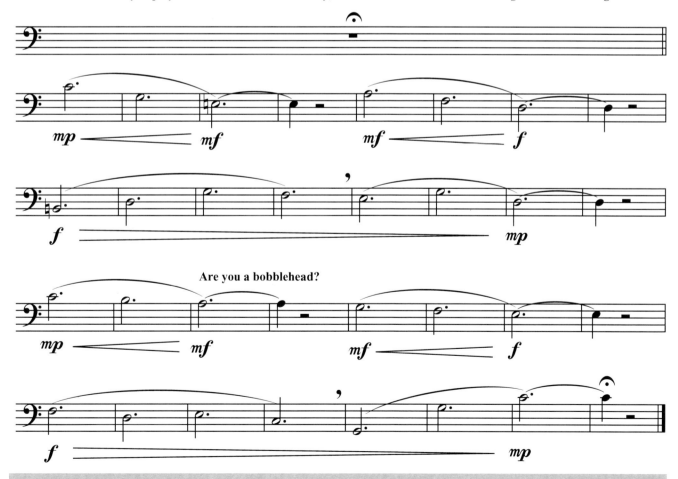

Are you a bobblehead?

4. Move your Ribs

Your lungs are not muscles. Your lungs are viscous organs which are surrounded by your twenty four ribs, twelve on each side, which wrap around your sides and are jointed to your spine in the back. In the front your ribs are attached to your flexible costal cartilage which, in turn, attaches to your sternum, or breast bone. Because of the joints in back and the cartilage in front, your ribs are extremely mobile. As you inhale, your ribs swing up and out, creating space in the thoracic cavity, which contains your lungs and heart. When the thoracic cavity gets larger, the air pressure is higher outside than in the cavity and the resulting disparity in air pressure causes air to rush in and fill the lung tissue.

Since your lungs are not muscles, they rely upon surrounding structures—the ribs, sternum, costal cartilage and diaphragm—to move them. Furthermore, you can't strengthen your lungs by exercising. This would be like saying you could strengthen your appendix by exercising!

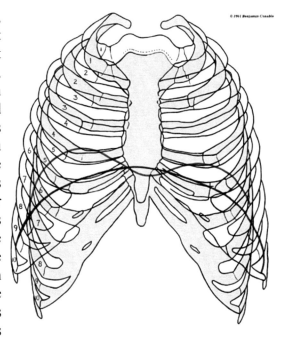

Because your lungs are surrounded by your ribs, sternum, costal cartilage and diaphragm, the amount these structures move determines the amount of air that can go into your lungs. As your ribs swing up and out, as in the image, they draw the viscous lung tissue with them. In between the ribs are two sets of muscles called intercostal muscles. The external intercostal muscles are responsible for swinging the ribs up and out as you inhale, and the internal intercostal muscles bring the ribs back down and in as you exhale. The intercostals move the ribs and this movement, along with the other important movements of breathing, results in the lungs filling up with air. It is important to understand that the movement of these structures causes air to fill the lungs, not the other way around! The more space which is created by the ribs moving, the more the lung tissue can fill up with air, therefore, when you allow generous amounts of rib movement, you can take in generous amounts of air.

Your arms are not attached to your ribs; they are suspended above your ribs. To allow your ribs their full range of motion, keep your elbows out of the way. Occasionally "flap your wings" gently as you play to make sure you have not collapsed your arm structure down onto your ribs. Try it now: while sitting in a balanced position with a free AO joint, bring your instrument into playing position and blow through it without making a sound. As you do so, try little "wing flapping" motions with your elbows. Experiment with bringing your elbows too low into your ribs and notice how this affects your breathing. Bring your elbows back out away from your body so your ribs can move and notice how much easier your breathing becomes. You can subtly "flap your wings" whenever you like as you play to insure that your arms are not inhibiting your rib movement. The movements can be so small that nobody sees them!

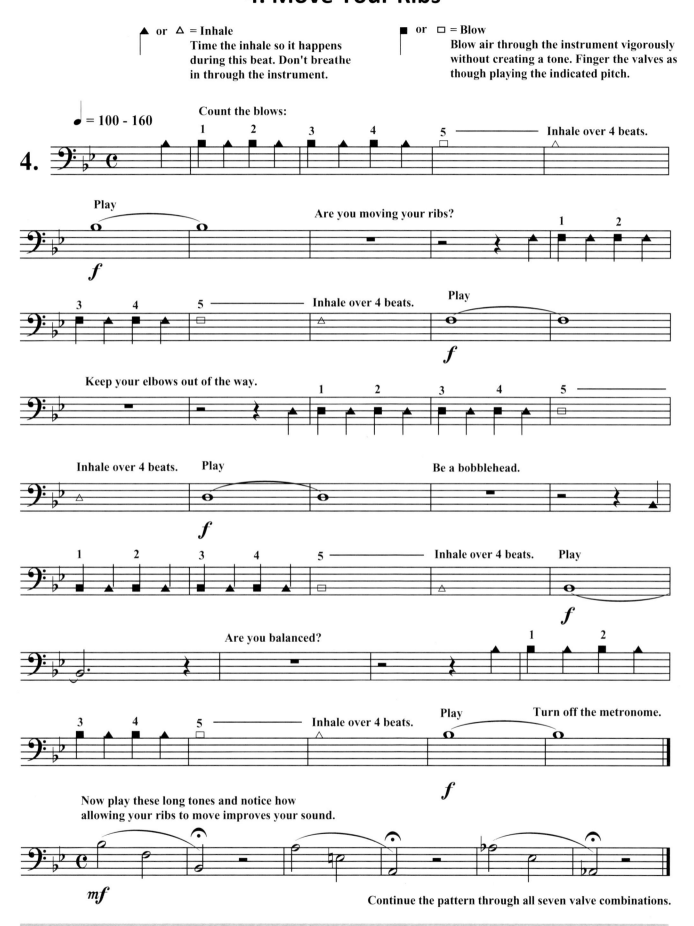

5. Allow Your Spine to Gather and Lengthen

As you inhale your spine gathers and as you exhale your spine lengthens, if you allow it. This important motion of breathing, known as spinal excursion, will only happen if you are balanced as you play. It will not happen if you try to make your back straight. After all, as you can see from the image, your spine is not straight; it has curves to absorb impact. It is also segmented into individual vertebra separated by soft, fluid-filled discs. This construction makes the spine strong yet flexible. Notice, also, that the spine is larger around at the bottom than at the top. This shape is because the lower part of your spine (or lumbar area) is responsible for bearing and delivering the weight of your torso, arms, instrument and head.

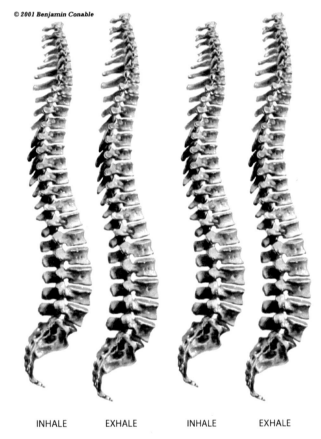

INHALE   EXHALE   INHALE   EXHALE

Spinal excursion is a powerful motion which coordinates the movements of breathing. It is an involuntary motion; we don't do it, we allow it. If you allow spinal excursion as you play, all the movements of breathing can occur in coordination with one another. If spinal excursion does not occur, the entire breathing process feels labored and your tone quality may not be as resonant as you would like, nor will you feel as buoyant as you should.

Spinal excursion will only occur if you are balanced. If you are balanced, your weight travels directly through your AO joint and downward through your moving spine. When your weight delivers through your core like this, your spine can move as in the image; with each inhalation, your spine gathers and with each exhalation it lengthens. This is the opposite of the compression some players create by squeezing air out of their body. When your spine gathers as you inhale, it brings your ribs closer together in the back, where they are jointed to your spine. This allows your ribs to move appropriately across their entire length. The two motions—rib excursion and spinal excursion—depend upon one another.

Feeling the subtle yet powerful motion of spinal excursion can be elusive to euphonium players. The sensation of the motion is one of internal buoyancy and support upon exhalation and you can learn to feel it if you do not overwhelm it with tense muscular effort as you play. If you don't feel it right away, don't be discouraged. The keys to observing spinal excursion are to be balanced and to cultivate an awareness of what is happening deep inside your body as you play. Be observant, be balanced and play free of tension, and you can learn to appreciate the enormous benefit of spinal excursion!

5. Allow Your Spine to Gather and Lengthen

6. The Truth About the Diaphragm

The diaphragm is a large dome-shaped structure which separates the thoracic cavity above from the abdominal cavity below. Your lungs rest on top of your diaphragm and, of course, the air goes in your lungs when you breathe. Air does not go below your diaphragm; in fact, if you believe air goes below your diaphragm, you are creating tension when you breathe. When you inhale, air behaves like air in your body, not like water. Air goes to all parts of the lungs immediately and equally. Air does not go to the bottom of the lungs first, as though filling up a glass of water. Trying to move air as if it were water to breathe creates tension and disrupts the natural movement of breathing.

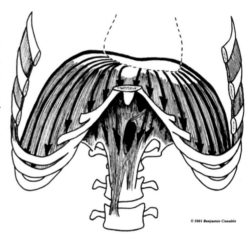

Your diaphragm does not have many sensory receptors so you can't directly feel it move inside your body. What you can feel are the primary motion of rib movement and the secondary motion of abdominal expansion. Your diaphragm and your external intercostals are the primary muscles of inspiration. As you inhale, the diaphragm contracts downward and the external intercostals swing the ribs up and out. The two movements depend upon one another because the diaphragm is attached to the ribs around the sides and the costal cartilage and the sternum in front.

The diaphragm contracts with every inhalation and relaxes with every exhalation. It is mainly muscle, although there is a circle of tendon in the middle called the central tendon (the white part in the image.) The muscle of the diaphragm contracts against the tendon, pulling it downward as you inhale. The phrase "breathe from the diaphragm" is confusing because it implies that there is some other way to breathe. It's like saying "smell with your nose"—there is no other way to do it!

The entire circumference of the diaphragm is connected all around to the inside of the sternum, the costal cartilage, the lowest ribs and the spine. Although you cannot touch the diaphragm, you can trace its position in the body. Try it now: looking at the illustration, trace the circumference of the diaphragm with your fingertips from the bottom of the sternum all the way around to your back. As you do so, bear in mind that the diaphragm domes well above the ribs that you are touching.

As you inhale, your diaphragm contracts, dragging the base of the lungs downward and increasing the circumference of the thoracic cavity. At the same time, the diaphragm pushes down hard on the contents of the abdominal cavity, squishing it out and down. This is where abdominal expansion comes from; it is a secondary motion which results from the diaphragm's downward motion. Pushing out your belly in an attempt to inhale does nothing more than create tension, so don't do it!

Since the diaphragm, ribs, costal cartilage and spine are connected, their motions depend upon one another. As the diaphragm makes its descent, the ribs swing up and out and the spine gathers. As the diaphragm makes its ascent, the ribs swing back down and in and the spine lengthens. All the motions happen together, not separated from one another. When you allow the motions to occur naturally, your breathing is organic and efficient, and your tone is resonant and free of tension.

7. Feel Support from Your Pelvic Floor

Beneath the abdominal cavity lies a network of muscles known as the pelvic floor. The pelvic floor is sometimes metaphorically referred to as a second diaphragm because of its importance in breathing.

As you inhale your thoracic diaphragm makes its descent and, in doing so, pushes down on the contents of the abdominal cavity. The organs contained in the abdominal cavity get squeezed by the motion of the diaphragm and are moved down and out. In order to allow the abdominal contents to move down and out and the diaphragm to make its full excursion, it's important to have a soft belly as you inhale. Musicians who keep their abdominal muscles continually contracted disrupt the movement of the diaphragm.

When the contents of the abdominal cavity flow out as you inhale, they also drive downward onto the pelvic floor, deepening its downward arc as in the image. This will only happen if you do not tighten up the muscles which comprise the pelvic floor. These are the muscles you would clench tightly if there were no bathroom around and you had to go.

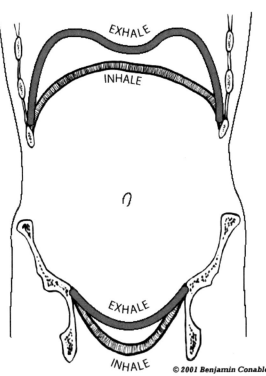

Upon exhalation, the thoracic diaphragm relaxes back up to its highly domed position and the pelvic floor springs back up to its original position. The springing of the pelvic floor back up is similar to stepping off a miniature trampoline. The springiness of the pelvic floor gives a sensation of internal support and buoyancy to your exhalation, if you are not clenching the muscles which comprise it.

The most common reason musicians can't feel their pelvic floor is that its subtle motion is overwhelmed by intense effort from the abdominal muscles. To feel support from your pelvic floor, have a soft belly and allow spinal excursion. In order to be aware of your soft belly and spinal excursion, you must become more sensitive to what is happening deep inside your body as you breathe and this is the key to discovering the sensation of support from your pelvic floor.

Playing euphonium is like a jeweler setting a fine stone. The activity is highly coordinated, requiring sensitivity and finesse, and the result is elegant and refined. Playing euphonium is not like weightlifting, which requires intense muscular effort and results in moving heavy objects. The best musicians do not work hard to create their art. They are sensitive to the powerful yet subtle motions of support from the pelvic floor and spinal excursion. They allow resonance to occur; they don't force resonance to occur.

7. Feel Support From Your Pelvic Floor

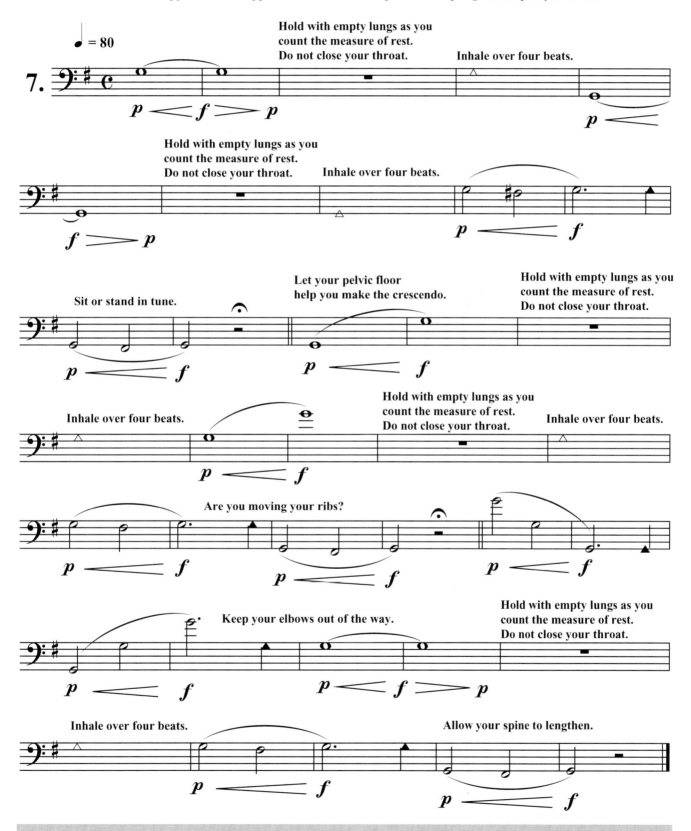

8. Exhalation and Elastic Recoil

We need to make a distinction between the muscular work of breathing and what happens to support the breath. The muscular work of inhaling is done by the intercostals (about twenty-five percent of the work) and the diaphragm (about seventy-five.) If this muscular work stopped, you would die. The subtle internal sensations of buoyant support for the breath, by contrast, come largely from elastic recoil throughout the torso accompanied by spinal lengthening on exhalation. The sensations come from a coordinated involuntary action of everything you see in the picture on this page. Unfortunately, some euphonium players think that intense muscular work in the muscles that have been removed in this picture is necessary to support the breath. These players typically equate making music with an athletic activity and, as a result, feel compelled to "muscle" their way through the music. This is unfortunate because these players are risking serious injury and ruining their chances for real support.

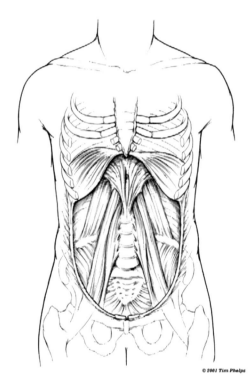

Elastic recoil is the tendency of tissue to rebound to its original shape. When your lungs are full of air, the abdominal cylinder, pelvic floor, lung tissue, costal cartilage and diaphragm have moved into a position other than neutral. When you exhale there is elastic recoil in all of these body parts as they seek their former neutral position. Elastic recoil occurs involuntarily every time you exhale and you can use elastic recoil to help support your tone, if you do not overwhelm it with unnecessary abdominal effort.

The abdominal wall is a layered cylinder of muscle surrounding the viscera; front, sides and back. When the diaphragm makes its descent as you inhale, the viscera are moved down against the pelvic floor and out against the entire abdominal cylinder. The pressure put on the abdominal cylinder by the viscera's motion outward and downward is equal in all directions. The viscera move outward against the entire cylinder and the movement should be felt all around, not just in front. Euphonium players who are preoccupied with abdominal motion in the front cheat themselves of the internal support available from the sides and back as the abdominal wall springs back to neutral upon exhalation.

Sighing is a good way to learn how to eliminate excess abdominal muscular effort and begin to appreciate elastic recoil. Try it now without your instrument: take a big breath and sigh, as though relieving the stress of a long day. When you play your instrument, imagine that each exhalation is a sigh enhanced with minimal muscular effort. As you play, be aware of the internal sensation of support which comes from elastic recoil and help it along just as much as you need to create the sound you want. What you need to do to support your tone will be different for every sound. How much effort you need depends upon the range and volume of the music. Do not assume that more muscular effort is necessarily better. After all, why work harder than you need to?

8. Exhalation and Elastic Recoil

○ = Finger the valves for the indicated note and "sigh" through your instrument without any vocal noise, as described in the text on the previous page.

For each played note, use minimal muscular effort. Support the tone but duplicate the feel of the sigh. Experiment with using as little effort as possible.

Throughout this activity, play at a comfortable, relaxed pace.
Do not use a metronome.

9a. Breathe All Over—Low Range

Some teachers say "breathe low" when teaching how to breathe. While there are certainly important breathing motions which occur low in the torso, the danger of thinking this way is that you might neglect the other important motions of breathing which occur higher in the body. Furthermore, as we have learned, the motions of breathing are all interconnected and they depend upon one another. When you breathe, don't just breathe low—breathe low, medium and high!

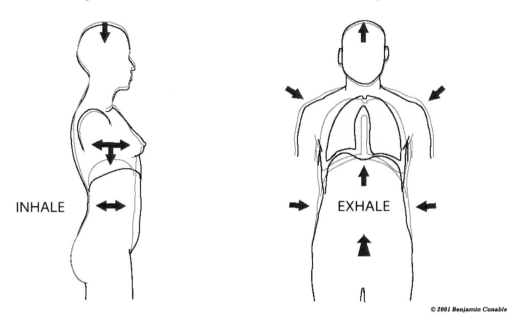

The individual motions of breathing are as follows: when you inhale, your external intercostal muscles contract moving the ribs up and out and your diaphragm contracts, pushing down on the contents of the abdominal cavity below. The contents of the abdominal cavity flow out and down, deepening the arc of the pelvic floor and causing abdominal expansion. At the same time, the spine gathers, bringing the ribs slightly closer together in the back. As this happens, the ribs swing up and out, creating space in the thoracic cavity which contains the lungs. The space causes inequality in air pressure between the thoracic cavity and the atmosphere outside the body, and air rushes in to fill the lungs and equalize the pressure.

Upon exhalation, the internal intercostal muscles contract moving the ribs back down and in and the diaphragm relaxes, seeking its former neutral highly domed position. At the same time, the ribs swing back down and in and the spine lengthens. The pelvic floor springs back up, helping to push the contents of the abdominal cavity up in a distinctive, tide-like motion. During exhalation, there is elastic recoil in the abdominal cylinder, pelvic floor, lung tissue, costal cartilage and diaphragm as these structures seek their neutral position of rest.

All of the individual movements of breathing coalesce into the singular, well coordinated and organic composite motion of breathing. The composite, sequential motion of breathing is complex but it needn't be confusing because, ultimately, musicians need only cooperate with nature to breathe well. Allow all the motions to occur free of tension and free of misunderstandings!

9a. Breathe All Over - Low Range

9b. Breathe All Over—High Range

Low notes require slow moving air and high notes require fast moving air. Along with these differences in air speed, there are corresponding differences in air quantity; low notes require a large quantity of air and high notes require less air. There is a continuum in between these extremes. If you have a note in the middle register, for example, it will require a medium amount of air moved at a medium speed. At any point in your range, you must use the right speed and quantity of air in order to achieve the sound you want. In addition to changes in range, changes in dynamics also require adjustments to the speed and quantity of the air. Obviously, louder notes require more air than softer notes. One must take care not to reduce the air flow too much for soft notes, however, because adequate breath support is still required in order to ensure a resonant tone.

A good analogy for the adjustments to the air speed and quantity is to compare the air to water flowing through a garden hose. If you turn on the water and hold the hose without covering the end with your thumb it creates a large quantity of water flowing slowly—the equivalent to playing a low note. If you put your thumb over the hole to squirt the water across the yard, there is less water flowing out of the hole and it is moving at a faster speed. This is the equivalent to playing a high note.

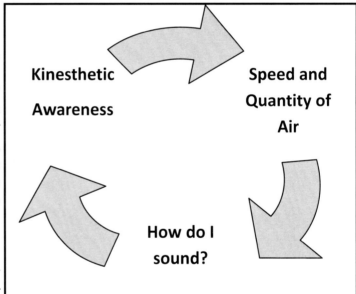

As you play, musical attributes such as range and dynamics are always changing. The better you are able to smoothly negotiate these changes, the better musician you are. An intimate knowledge of the air flow requirements at any given point in a phrase is important to success. Some euphonium players have an instinctive understanding of air flow but others need to learn these details.

An important tool ignored by many struggling euphonium players for monitoring subtle differences in air speed and quantity is kinesthesia, the sensory mode which enables us to perceive our movements. Kinesthesia tells us about the size, shape and position of a body part, the quality of its motion and its interaction with other body parts. You have already been encouraged to use your kinesthesia to discover the subtle yet powerful motions of spinal excursion and support from the pelvic floor, among other movements.

Use your kinesthetic awareness to carefully observe how you are using your air. Subtle changes in air quality are accompanied by subtle changes in the quality of the breathing motion and produce slightly different sounds. A heightened kinesthetic awareness will allow you to collect more information about the speed and quantity of your air and this information will help you refine your sound. Form healthy connections between the quality of your movements and the refinement of your sound.

10. Let the Air Drive Your Tongue

Your tongue is comprised of a network of many little muscles; it is not just one big muscle. Its construction allows you to move the front of the tongue without work in the back of the tongue. When you articulate, move the tip of your tongue (approximately the first ¼ inch) as if saying "ta" ("da" for softer articulations). The back of your tongue should not be working unless you are multiple tonguing.

As you blow and articulate, imagine that the tongue is a speed boat bouncing off the water, which is your air. If you count on the air to drive your tongue in this way, you don't need to work as hard with your tongue and you can achieve light, effortless articulations.

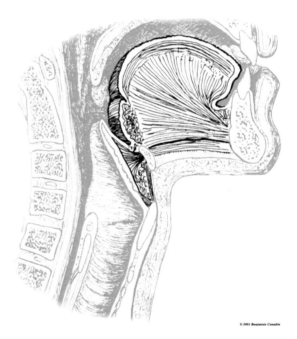

The back third of the tongue is vertical, as you can see from the image. This part of the tongue also forms the front wall of a space which is known as the pharyngeal space. When we blow air to produce our tone on euphonium, the air must travel through this space. In fact, one could regard the pharyngeal space as a resonating cavity for a euphonium player. If the pharyngeal space is relaxed, the tone is resonant. If the pharyngeal space closes either because tensed neck muscles drive the vertebra into the space or because the tongue contracts backward into it, the tone quality suffers.

Since the back third of the tongue serves as the front wall of the pharyngeal space, it is important to avoid engaging this part of the tongue unless you are multiple tonguing. Understanding the tongue's construction is essential to accomplishing this. If you believe your tongue is a single big muscle, you will have no choice but to move the entire tongue with every articulation because you will expect a sensation of work in the entire tongue rather than just in part of the tongue. Of course, if you do this, you will close off the pharyngeal space and your tone quality will suffer.

Remember, the tongue is comprised of little muscles working in networks independent of each other. This construction allows the tongue to move in a seemingly endless variety of ways, including allowing the front to move without involving the back. Furthermore, when the back of your tongue is not involved, your pharyngeal space is open and free and your tone is correspondingly resonant. When these conditions are present, the air flows freely through the pharyngeal space and can effectively drive the tongue like a speed boat. Not only is your tone free and beautiful but your articulations are nimble and easy!

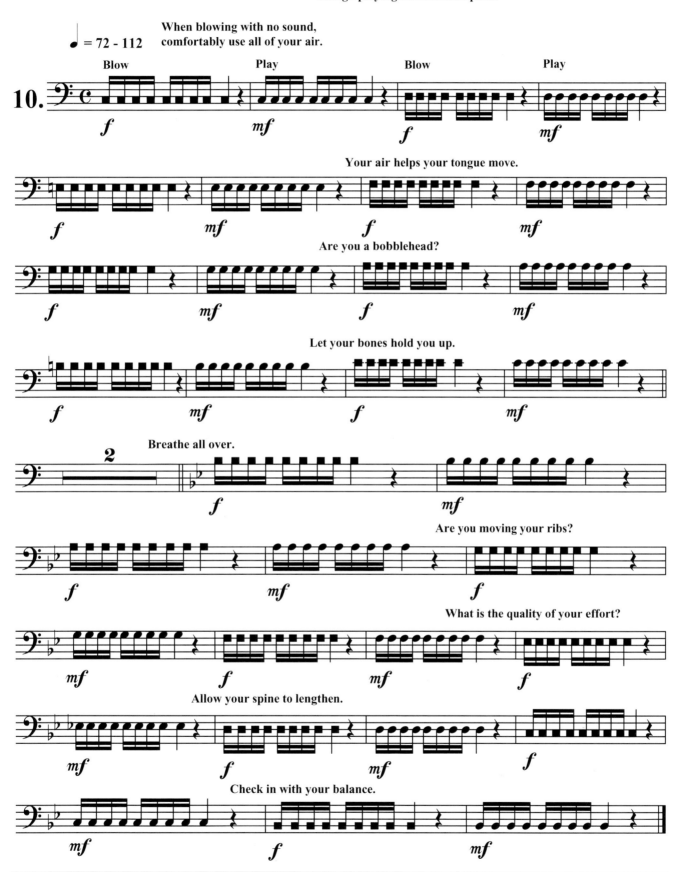

11a. Blow Freely as You Change Notes—Slow

Sometimes our breathing suffers when we play technical passages or when we have to change registers. Ironically, moving air through the notes is precisely what will make these passages sound better! Our goal is to remain free of tension even though we have to negotiate fast notes or register changes.

Remember that balance is an ongoing, lively attribute. Balance accommodates movements of all kinds including the movements of breathing. Balance accommodates movements at the AO joint and it accommodates subtle movements of your instrument. To make music is to move and the best musicians have freedom of movement available to them at all times because they are balanced.

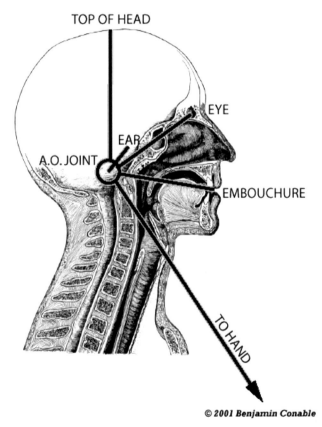
© 2001 Benjamin Conable

To play technical passages well or to change registers effectively, continue to be balanced in spite of the technical difficulty. As you play these passages, allow your AO joint to stay free. A free AO joint will help ensure that you remain balanced as you negotiate the difficult passages and that you are able to support the tone with the air flow.

In order to remain balanced as you play technical passages or change registers, it is important to know that the embouchure is below the AO joint, as is clear in the image. You should allow your instrument to be freely responsive to any subtle movements required of your embouchure as you play. If you need to tilt your instrument up or down or side to side as you change registers, you should do so on a lower plane than your AO joint. A free AO joint will allow you the freedom to subtly tilt your instrument in cooperation with delicate changes in your embouchure. As your instrument moves in cooperation with your embouchure, you may also move at your AO joint but only if the joint is free and only if you understand that the joint is slightly higher than your embouchure.

Musicians move for a living. The best musicians have freedom of movement available at all times. They play free of tension because they are aware of the relationship between their AO joint and their embouchure.

11a. Blow Freely as You Change Notes - Slow

11b. Blow Freely as You Change Notes—Fast

In order to blow freely as you play fast notes, it is important to know that your arms are not attached to your ribs. Your arms are suspended above your ribs by a network of fascia, tendons and ligaments. Because of this construction, your ribs can move independent from your arms.

Here is an image of the collarbones, shoulder blades and ribs looking down from above. The spine is at the top of the image and the sternum is at the bottom. Notice that the collarbones are not attached to the ribs in front and that the shoulder blades are not attached to the ribs in back. Your collarbones and shoulder blades are attached to one another but they are not attached to your ribs, therefore, both the ribs and the arm structure can move freely as you play.

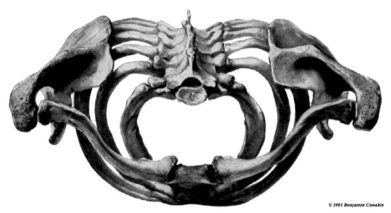

The place where your collarbones and shoulder blades join the rest of your bony structure is in the front, where the collarbones are jointed to the sternum. At the spot where each collarbone meets the sternum there is a joint known as the sterno-clavicular, or SC, joint. Take a moment and find it now, using the images as guides.

Touch your right collarbone with the fingers of your left hand. Walk back and forth on your collarbone to understand where it begins and ends. Now find the point at which your collarbone joins your sternum, the highlighted area in the image. This is your SC joint. As you are touching your SC joint, swim with your right arm using your full range of motion. Do you feel your collarbone moving in its attachment at the sternum? You should!

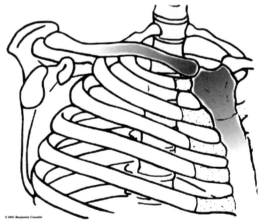

The SC joints are the only bone-to-bone attachments between your arms and the rest of your body. Your arms are not connected to your ribs at your sides and your shoulder blades are not connected to your ribs in the back. Your SC joints are the point of reference for all of your arm movements; therefore, free SC joints allow free and full arm movements.

With each breath, your ribs swing up and out as you inhale and down and in as you exhale. This rib motion occurs regardless of what your arms are doing as you play, if your arms are not collapsed over your ribs. Take care that you do not inhibit rib motion while negotiating fast or difficult technical passages. After all, moving the air through the notes is the key to making the technical passages clean and the air can't move if the ribs don't move!

11b. Blow Freely as You Change Notes - Fast

12. Quality of Effort and the Valsalva Maneuver

Playing euphonium is a highly coordinated activity requiring large attention and small muscular effort. Fine euphonium players are more like dancers than football players. They are more like Olympic divers than Olympic wrestlers. How would you describe the quality of your music-making effort? Do you approach your instrument with the highly coordinated refinement of a dancer or with the overwhelming muscular effort of a weightlifter? The quality of your movements determines the quality of your sound and if your music-making movements are tense, your sound will be tense. If your music-making movements are free, your sound will be free.

Euphonium players who have a muscular approach to playing their instrument can experience the Valsalva maneuver as they play. The Valsalva maneuver is the body's way of consolidating strength by closing the throat and pushing against this closure with the abdominal muscles. When the Valsalva maneuver is used, we gain leverage for activities such as lifting heavy items, defecation or, for women, childbirth. The Valsalva maneuver is a bodily function and we are all capable of using it for these and other activities when it is needed. We must take care not to regard euphonium playing as an activity which requires this sort of muscular effort because if we do, the body may involuntarily apply the Valsalva maneuver as we play.

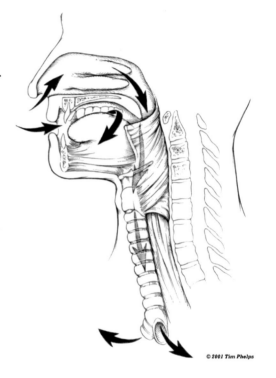

The image on this page shows the pharyngeal muscles that lie on three sides of the pharyngeal space with arrows to show where the air goes. This space is a resonating cavity for euphonium players and it is surrounded by the muscles which close in Valsalva. When the muscles in the image contract during Valsalva, there is a corresponding reduction in the amount of resonance in the tone quality because the space is reduced.

© 2001 Tim Phelps

Euphonium players must understand that the muscles surrounding the pharyngeal space are part of the digestive system; they are not respiratory muscles. Take a moment now to swallow and feel these muscles contract. The muscles of swallowing are not used to play euphonium; we do not swallow air. Euphonium players who suffer from engagement of the Valsalva maneuver while playing produce a thin, choked tone quality, have trouble starting notes on time and may even grunt as they articulate or change registers. It is possible to have varying degrees of throat closure, or Valsalva; even a little throat closure is detrimental to euphonium playing. The best players have necks which are completely free of tension with absolutely no evidence of Valsalva closure.

To produce a free tone quality, have a free neck. To have a free neck, be a balanced bobblehead and play like a dancer, not a weightlifter!

12. Quality of Effort and the Valsalva Maneuver

▲ = Inhale
Time the inhale so it happens during this beat. Don't breathe in through the instrument.

☐ = Blow
Blow air through the instrument without creating a tone. Finger the valves as though playing the indicated pitch.

♩ = 72   In this activity, blow gently. Never force sound to occur.

*Gradually allow a tone to occur as you are blowing. It is acceptable for the tone to start after the asterisk.

**Allow sound to happen.
Don't force sound to happen.**

Are you balanced at your AO joint?

Are you balanced at your lumbar spine?

What is the quality of your effort?

Be a bobblehead.

Keep your elbows out of the way.

13. Monitor Your Air Gauge

To play well, learn to monitor how you use your air to create your tone. You can notice how much air you are using, how fast the air is moving, and how much air is left, if you cultivate sensitivity to these attributes.

Throughout this book you have been encouraged to cultivate sensitivity to all the subtle movements of breathing. Now that you are sensitive to these movements, you can use this sensitivity to monitor how you are using your air. Ask yourself questions such as: how fast is the air moving and is this speed giving me the sound I want? What quantity of air is being used relative to the speed? How much air is left in my lungs? Will I make the phrase? These questions are important because the answers to them will determine your sound. The more sensitive you are to your air gauge, the more subtle your adjustments can be as you make music on your instrument. You can use your tactile sense to feel the air move through the sensitive tissue in your nose and mouth. Sensitivity to the quality of the movement of air across these areas provides valuable information as you monitor your air gauge.

Air Gauge

- How much air is left?
- What quantity of air am I using?
- What speed of air am I using?

Am I getting the sound I want?

Changes in dynamics or range require corresponding changes in air speed and quantity. When you consider these special musical situations and the air needs of a euphonium player, the "air equation" can become quite complicated! In order to simplify the process, it's best to think of ordering air based upon the needs of the music and reinforcing the sound with your sensitivity to your air gauge. Notice the speed and quantity of your air flow and be aware of how much air is left in your lungs.

Never try to push all of the air out of your lungs because there is always residual air which remains in the lungs. When the new air comes in, it mixes with the residual air and maintains equilibrium between the amount of carbon dioxide and the amount of oxygen in your lungs, and ensures that your lungs will not collapse. Attempting to push the last bit of air out of your lungs will cause tension in your body and your tone will suffer. It is equally important to finish your breath comfortably. Residual air will remain in the lungs if you are comfortably empty so there is no need to feel that you must preserve residual air. Sensitivity to your air gauge combined with kinesthetic awareness will inform you of your comfort level. You should not feel as though you are squeezing air out, nor should you feel that you have too much air left over at the ends of phrases.

Strive to produce the sound you want and allow the air to feed that sound with freedom and ease. Monitor your air gauge to ensure you are using your air efficiently and order air based upon the needs of the music.

Summary

Music is movement. The quality of a euphonium player's movements determines the quality of the sound. Free movements create free sounds and tense movements create tense sounds. Breathing movements which are free of tension happen when we move in cooperation with how we are built. In other words, if we know how we are supposed to move to breathe, we will move freely and our sound will be resonant. If our movements do not cooperate with the reality of how we are built, our sound will be full of tension and our resonance will suffer.

The individual motions of breathing are as follows: when you inhale, your external intercostal muscles contract moving the ribs up and out and your diaphragm contracts, increasing the thoracic circumference and pushing down on the contents of the abdominal cavity below. The contents of the abdominal cavity flow out and down, deepening the arc of the pelvic floor and causing abdominal expansion. At the same time, the spine gathers, bringing the ribs slightly closer together in the back. As this happens, the ribs swing up and out, creating space in the thoracic cavity which contains the lungs. The space causes inequality in air pressure between the thoracic cavity and the atmosphere outside the body and air rushes in to fill the lungs and equalize the pressure.

Upon exhalation, the internal intercostal muscles contract moving the ribs back down and in and your diaphragm relaxes, seeking its former neutral highly domed position. At the same time, the ribs swing back down and in and the spine lengthens. The pelvic floor springs back up, helping to push the contents of the abdominal cavity up in a distinctive, tide-like motion. During exhalation, there is elastic recoil in the abdominal cylinder, pelvic floor, lung tissue, costal cartilage and diaphragm as these structures seek their neutral position of rest.

All of the individual movements of breathing coalesce into the singular, well coordinated and organic composite motion of breathing. The composite, sequential motion of breathing is complex but it needn't be confusing because, ultimately, musicians need only cooperate with nature to breathe well. When you play, monitor your air gauge to ensure you are using your air suitably to meet the needs of the music. Your understanding of breathing works in the background, right alongside your understanding of music theory and music history.

On the following page is a flow study, an etude which can be considered the capstone experience of this book. Flow means moving the air smoothly through the phrase. Flow means creating maximum resonance with minimum effort. Flow also means blowing a steady stream of air through the phrase regardless of the movement of the valves. As you play the flow study, pay attention to your sound and ask yourself the following questions: Is the tone quality resonant? Are the note changes smooth? Is the phrasing natural and beautiful? All of these qualities depend upon efficient air flow—the very attribute this book seeks to cultivate. Your knowledge of breathing is a global improvement to your playing and will improve your sound in everything you play, not just a particular etude or excerpt. The time spent learning about breathing will continue to pay dividends long after you complete the reading and activities in this book. Come back to these pages often to reinforce your knowledge of breathing.

Flow Study

Flow means moving the air smoothly through the phrase.
Flow means creating *maximum resonance with minimum effort*.
Flow means blowing a steady stream of air through the phrase
regardless of the movement of the valves.

$\halfnote = \pm 66$ Choose a tempo at which the phrases are comfortable in one breath.

For more Flow Studies, try:

FLOW STUDIES→

Euphonium Edition

David Vining

Preface by Kelly Thomas

available at:

www.mountainpeakmusic.com